101 Substance Abuse Recovery Tips

LifeTips Book Series

By Blythe Landry
Substance Abuse Recovery Expert Guru
LifeTips

LifeTips
Move Up In Life.
LifeTips Book Series
Boston, Massachusetts

LIFETIPS PRESIDENT: Byron White
BOOK SERIES EDITOR: Melanie Nayer

All inquires should be addressed to:

LifeTips.com, Inc.
101 Book Series
One First Avenue
Building 34, Suite 200
Charlestown, MA 02129
(617) 886-9001
http://www.LifeTips.com

International Standard Book No. 978-1-60275-029-6

Table of Contents

A Note from the Editor

Many people view drug abuse and addiction as a social problem. Drug abusers are often referred to as "weak" and "helpless," and most commonly associated with the modern-day criminal. However, drug and alcohol abuse plagues even the wealthiest, smartest and secure individuals.

The National Institute on Drug Abuse (NIDA) supports more than 85 percent of the world's research on the health aspects of drug abuse and addiction and addresses some of the most vital questions about drug abuse including heredity causes to managed care to community outreach research. No matter how you look at it, however, drug abuse and addiction affects many Americans and in turn, has a damaging effect on our society and local communities.

As you'll learn in this tip book, addiction begins when an individual makes the choice to use drugs. But as Blythe Landry explains in this tip book for recovering addicts, addiction is more than just "drug use," it's a mental state of mind. Those addicted to drugs have a hard time just quitting, and often find themselves searching different avenues to feed their drug cravings. The bottom line: treatment is needed to end this addictive behavior.

It's up to parents, teachers, adults and health professionals to continue to educate on the dangers of drug abuse, and with the help of organizations like the National Institute on Drug Abuse (NIDA) and books like this one, we can continue to make progress in the war on drugs.

Melanie Nayer
LifeTips Editor

A Note from the Author

Addiction is a life-threatening illness that is both under-researched and often misunderstood. It is my intention in writing this book that those persons who are confused about addiction and/or how to seek help will gain knowledge and comfort. I also intend this book for the healthcare professionals who are looking for a place to begin the process of understanding their clients. My hope is that after reading this book those same people will seek out additional resources that are suggested throughout this text.

This is only one resource intended to draw attention to the addiction dilemma and encourage people to seek additional support and resources. My work as a therapist with clients suffering from severe mental illness and substance abuse has not only inspired me to help others through their struggles, but has humbled and changed me most profoundly.

I hope that I can provide the world with even a semblance of the bravery, strength, lessons, and beauty that these clients and the following people have brought into my life: JL, LMK, NR, WB, GM, NE, CS, ME, KB, DW, MN, my boys, my extended family network in Chicago and New York, the staff/faculty/friends of Inner-City Teaching Corps, Loyola University, Jewish Family and Community Services, Lakeshore Hospital and, of course the Landry Family, and the Stepping Up family.

Blythe Landry
LifeTips Expert Guru

1| Alcohol Dependence And Abuse

The first important element of beginning treatment for any type of addiction, including alcoholism, is to arm yourself with the facts. One of the best places to begin is with the book, *Diagnostic and Statistical Manual of Mental Disorders,* 4th Edition (more affectionately known as the DSMIV). This book is the go-to manual for all professionals dealing with any mental disorder and lists all the facts and symptoms regarding every single mental illness in existence. *Alcohol Intoxication, Alcohol Dependence* and *Alcohol Abuse* are each listed and defined in this book. A person who has trouble with their drinking or cannot stop drinking despite a strong desire and his/her best intended efforts can begin here. Notated symptoms, such as *"a persistent desire or unsuccessful efforts to cut down or control drinking"* (symptom of *Alcohol Dependence)* can lead to an informed decision about whether or not you need help with your drinking.

2| Alcohol Detox

One of the characteristics of alcoholism is that the "alcoholic" will suffer withdrawal symptoms when he/she ceases use. There are physiological and psychological consequences. Here, we will focus on the physiology of the disease. In late stage alcoholism a person may not be able to go more than an hour or so without his/her "fix." Some withdrawal symptoms are shakes, nausea, anxiety, and even hallucinations According to *Substance Abuse Counseling: Theory and Practice (third edition)* by P. Stevens and R. Smith, "..in severe cases, seizures, delirium tremors, cardiovascular collapse, death." Detox from alcoholism is the only form of substance abuse detox that can lead to death. Simply put, this is because alcohol can and does affect almost every organ of the body. The liver, which is the organ that detoxifies the body, is the most affected organ. Because of such potentially serious implications of the detox process you should never consider attempting to detox from alcohol alone. If you are ready to quit drinking, it is crucial that you check into a treatment facility with medical staff trained in this area.

3| Alcohol Rehabilitation: Getting Started

Alcohol detox is only the preliminary phase of alcohol rehabilitation. Alcoholism is a disease that permeates more than just the life of the alcoholic; its effects manifest themselves in the lives of family, friends, coworkers, and acquaintances. Rehabilitation from alcoholism is a life-long journey. So just like one would gather information about his/her disease if it were diabetes or asthma, the same is required to determine effective treatment choices for recovery from alcoholism.

A good place to begin is with the American Academy of Family Physicians website. The highlighted article, titled "Alcohol Related Problems: Recognition and Intervention," by Burge and Schneider, gives helpful information about the effects of alcohol on the body and mind and offers helpful question/answer techniques to determine the severity of one's alcohol dilemma.

Start here to determine which kind of early intervention will be most effective for you. It is also recommended that you ask a very close relative or friend to go through this information with you. This person will care enough about you to be honest about how they perceive the severity of your drinking problem.

4| Alcohol Rehabilitation: What to Expect

The first part of rehabilitation must include medical and possibly psychological attention. Physical and mental examination will be required. It is suggested, as stated in the detox section, that you check into an inpatient drug/rehab facility to get that initial push towards recovery. Be prepared to answer questions about your medical history, past lifestyle, behavioral patterns, relationships and use. This is not to be invasive, but rather to get a full bio-psychosocial picture of you so that optimal treatment can be provided.

You cannot recover from alcoholism by simply reading a list of tips such as those offered here-although reading this is a good place to begin and to tap into more expansive resources.

5| Are You Ready For Recovery?

Rehabilitation from alcoholism is not possible unless the alcoholic is willing and ready to change. It may seem odd to you if you have lost your job, your family and everything you thought you loved and you still don't want to quit drinking. This is a normal part of the disease. Read that again: *this is a normal part of the disease.* If you really want some help, there is hope. If you are reading this and wondering if you are the only person out there who feels this "crazy," then you are mistaken. There is a world of people who have felt as you do and who have made drastic life changes. And that change is available to everyone who wants it. But before you read on, ask yourself:

- Have I had enough alcohol?
- Am I at a point where I cannot move forward?
- Are I sick of doing the same things and expecting different results, only to find myself flat out on my back again?
- Have I heard from enough people that my behavior makes them sad, or even that they want to keep me out of their lives?

If you answered "yes" to these questions, then you may be to embark on the very difficult process, yet ultimately rewarding journey of true recovery from alcoholism.

6| Dealing With Psychological Effects of Alcohol

Alcohol is a disease that manifests itself both physically and psychologically. Here we will deal with the psychological components of the disease. Simply put: alcohol abuse messes up your thinking. Your emotions are displaced, distorted and deviant. When you are finally at the point where you want to stop drinking, you may feel helpless, hopeless, and devastated. *The Big Book of Alcoholics Anonymous* refers to this as "the jumping off point," where you are too miserable to live and too afraid to die. You will feel irritable, anxious, exhausted, ashamed, fearful and maybe hopeful, but all at the same time. You do not have to experience this alone. At this point, it is necessary to arm yourself with a network of support.

It is suggested that you attend Alcoholics Anonymous meetings (in major cities like Chicago there are 4,000 meetings a week). It is also recommended that a medical doctor, a therapist and a network of sober, supportive friends be used for assistance during this time. You are not the professional here, so seek help from others who understand you. Trying these new tools will help. You cannot think your way into a new way of acting, but you can act your way into a new way of thinking and feeling.

7| Emotional Withdrawal From Alcoholism

Once you decide to stop drinking, emotional withdrawal can be quite severe. Alcohol has most likely become your best friend. It is the one thing the alcoholic can always rely upon to take away his/her feelings. This "best friend," though, is the equivalent of a pal who would sleep with your wife or husband, steal all your money and then murder you in the end. Even though the alcohol was the furthest thing from a friend in reality, you will still grieve.

Many experts believe that a person's emotional development is stunted at the time of use onset. If you have been drinking since you were a teenager, you will likely have a lot of energy and feelings with which to cope. To channel this energy - this combination of misery and euphoria you will experience in early sobriety - stay active and engage in activities that increase your self-esteem. Learn to run. Go for walks. Take up visual art. Join a cooking class (eating sugar is recommended, if you aren't allergic, diabetic, or a member of Overeaters Anonymous). Take a different route to work. All of these things will replace your negative behaviors and emotions with more positive ones, as well as take up the time you would have formerly spent drinking.

8| Gaining Back Your Life

Alcoholism takes away your dignity, your self-esteem, your health and your life. The good news is that there is help. After the preliminary stages of rehabilitation, such as detox, medical and psychological attention, one journey to consider is becoming a member of Alcoholics Anonymous.

If you would like a chance at a truly successful, positive lifestyle then it is essential you surround yourself with people who understand your disease, and AA is one place that offers that possibility. It is recommended, too, that you find a sponsor and work the 12 steps of Alcoholics Anonymous. If you do not obtain some type of support network, you will most likely drink again.

In order to find an AA meeting place that is comfortable for you, visit at least five or six different meetings before you make a decision as to which one works for you. All meetings are different and focus on different aspects of recovery. Additionally, it is recommended that you find a sponsor to help you work the 12-steps right away.

For more recovery options, go to http://www.niaaa.nih.gov/ (National Institute on Alcohol Abuse and Alcoholism).

9| Suggestions For Medical Interactions

Sometimes it is recommended that those in early recovery from alcoholism seek psychological support. Many people drink to "self-medicate" from otherwise intolerable feelings, such as anxiety, depression, and even mania or hallucinations. These things may not go away once you get sober. While internists are an excellent resource for people struggling with strictly medical problems, and can be useful to you in retrieving your physical strength, it is recommended that you seek psychiatric support for any concerns regarding your mental health.

It is highly recommended that you do research on psychiatrists who specifically have experience in the area of alcoholism. Addiction is largely under-researched and misunderstood-even in the medical field. It is crucial that you examine your options prior to treatment so that you can receive the highest and most appropriate level of care.

10| Your Window of Recovery Opportunity

The chances of seeking help for alcoholism are optimal during your the moments of awareness (typically right after an embarrassing episode). After a few hours of obsessing about the mistakes you made while drinking, your mind will quickly convince you to pick up a drink to satiate the shame. This "shame cycle" is part of the disease that keeps giving you permission to drink and to engage in self-destruction so that you have an excuse to drink again and again. Doesn't make much sense, does it? That is precisely why it is important to seek help fast when you are thinking sanely.

It is suggested that the morning after your last episode, when you are overwhelmed with discomfort, that you call a local AA office and ask someone for help. This way, someone else's clearer thinking can get to you before your disease tells you to cover up the guilt and shame with another secretive self-destructive behavior.

It is also suggested that you seek medical attention immediately if you have a history of frequent use. See detox section for the importance of this decision.

11| Crack/Cocaine Rehabilitation: Early Stages

While crack/cocaine are different forms of the same substance, and certainly not always used in conjunction, they will be combined here to address treatment concerns. The research regarding crack/cocaine use and effective treatment is still in its infancy, however, some useful determinations have been made. It is known that complete abstinence from drug use after detox is most effective in avoiding recurring abuse.

Some data suggests that relapse prevention models and cognitive-behavioral therapy for outpatient treatment is more effective than insight-focused psychotherapy. It is usually recommended that residential treatment and intensive outpatient support take place in the first stages of rehabilitation.

The research regarding crack/cocaine use and effective treatment is still in its infancy and inconclusive. However, some useful determinations have been made. It is known that the decision to opt for complete abstinence from drug use after detox is the most effective tool for avoiding recurring (and potentially life-threatening) abuse.

12| Crack/Cocaine Rehabilitation: Gaining a Network of Support

Once you've given up crack/cocaine and committed yourself to life-long abstinence, you will need a network of support. It's important to know that despite ceasing use, you will likely still experience distorted thinking and addictive tendencies. The unfortunate side is that you will always have the disease of addiction. The good news is that unlike a terminal prognosis for a cancer patient, there is a solution to your problem.

It is suggested that you quickly obtain a network of support through Cocaine Anonymous and that you attend as many meetings per week that you were using your drug of choice. You should put as much, if not more, effort into maintaining your sobriety as you did maintaining your addiction. It was said by one recovering alcoholic "My friend is dying from cancer, and I bet if he had the choice to either attend regular meetings and live or to keep his disease and die, he would opt for the meetings. Unlike me, he doesn't get that choice." Becoming a part of a recovery group can be that simple of a decision for which one can practice gratitude, rather than self-pity. This kind of thinking will seem strange at first, as the addict mind is dubious, defiant and self-centered to the extreme. In time, however, such reflection and acceptance can become second nature.

13| Crack/Cocaine Rehabilitation in the Workplace

If you have been at the same job for an extended period of time, it is likely that your boss/peers know about your drug problem. If not, the decision to disclose your medical/mental health issues in the workplace is always a tricky one. Refer to trusted resources -- such as medical/psychological journals, instead of pop culture magazines -- for support in making this decision.

A great article to begin with is "Should I Tell the Boss? Disclosing a Psychiatric Condition in the Workplace" by Diana Ballon, from *Journal of Addiction and Mental Health* 4(1), 13. It's also suggested that you ask other recovering addicts whom you respect and trust about their opinions and experiences on such matters.

14| Additional Support for Drug Rehabilitation from Crack/Cocaine

Cocaine Anonymous, while suggested as the primary mode of long-term treatment for this addiction, is not always a large fellowship and may not even exist in some smaller cities. Narcotics Anonymous is another option, but may also be difficult to find. However, if you're addicted to cocaine, there is a strong likelihood you are also addicted to alcohol (or at least cannot use alcohol because it results in you using/abusing cocaine again).

There are Alcoholics Anonymous meetings virtually everywhere. At first, it is suggested you go to "open" AA meetings so you won't feel like an intruder if you haven't found your addiction focuses on alcohol.

You can find out if a meeting is "open" by looking in a local AA directory or at http://www.alcoholics-anonymous.org, where there will be some indicator of the meeting status (such as an "o" or the word "open") after the listing of the meeting. Once you feel comfortable in your support network, you will find plenty of other men and women in AA who also struggle with crack/cocaine (or view that as their primary addiction). They will be of invaluable support during your battle with crack/cocaine recovery.

15| Crack/Cocaine Abuse and Mental Illness

Addiction is considered a mental illness according to the *Diagnostic and Statistical Manual of Mental Disorders (IV)*. There is a very strong link between all addictive processes and other mental illnesses. The research is inconclusive regarding which problem occurs first and it may be different for each person. Depression (or depressive symptoms) is very common prior to use, during use and after use cessation. If you feel sad, lethargic, empty (a very common expression used by addicts), lonely, worthless, hopeless, or agitated, then you may be suffering from depression. If these symptoms are severe and persist over time, you may be experiencing a Major Depressive Episode.

It is recommended that you work with a therapist/psychiatrist to determine if you need psychological or even medical support to battle this depression. Again, it is important to work with a professional who is well-versed in the disease of addiction so that you receive optimal support. If you are feeling suicidal, homicidal, or having any hallucinations, it is crucial that you check yourself into an inpatient psychiatric facility to meet your immediate needs.

16| Crack/Cocaine Withdrawal

If you have stopped using crack/cocaine, it's important to know about withdrawal symptoms. After prolonged use, you may begin to experience such symptoms as chronic fatigue, increased appetite, insomnia or extreme agitation within only a few hours of your last use. The closer your withdrawal symptoms are to your last time of use, the more severe your addiction is.

If you are experiencing these severe symptoms, you are in serious danger both physically and psychologically. At this point, the drug is no longer achieving that long-term high and you will never be able to consume enough of the drug to make you feel better again.

You should receive medical attention at a drug rehab facility to assure a safe detoxification/withdrawal process, and follow it with an appointment with a therapist, an internist and a series of 12-Step Meetings. A nutritionist may also be helpful in rehabilitating your immune system, which is probably very weak.

17| How To Respond To Crack/Cocaine Intoxication

Cocaine can be referred to as snow, flake, lady and blow, to name a few. Crack is simply cocaine in smokeable form. This drug is highly addictive and you can show signs of intoxication, or become addicted to crack/cocaine after one use. If you use the drug and show signs of intoxication, such as excessive perspiration, chills, vomiting, chest pain, or muscular weakness, you MUST seek help immediately. Some options include:

-Checking yourself into an inpatient medical unit to receive help in detoxing your body.

-Going to the closest emergency room and being honest about the fact that you are currently high on cocaine/crack. Let them know that you fear you are in trouble and that you want support. They are required to give you medical attention, and they will most likely refer you to another facility to deal with the psychological components of the addiction after you are safely detoxed.

18| Medication and Crack/Cocaine Rehabilitation

The evidence is inconclusive regarding the use of medication in the assistance of crack/cocaine rehabilitation. During drug rehab, a prescription for benzodiazepines (i.e. Xanax, Ativan) is sometimes recommended. This decision is usually based on the physician's desire to ease unpleasant withdrawal symptoms, such as insomnia or severe anxiety. The dilemma is that people can develop a dependency on this class of drugs and they do not alleviate the long-term issues you will grapple with regarding anxiety. They may alleviate short-term discomfort, but you may also find yourself addicted to yet another substance.

Withdrawal from benzodiazepines is sometimes worse than detox from other drugs. While you should always consult with a doctor for your final decision, it is strongly recommended that you work with a doctor who specializes in the treatment of addictions.

19| More Information About Crack/Cocaine Use and Rehabilitation

Like any other disease, it is suggested that you become very aware of the psychological and physiological effects that crack/cocaine has on your body, as well as the most recommended treatments for successful rehabilitation. One good (and free) place to start is the National Institute on Drug Abuse website (http://www.nida.nih.gov/Infofacts/cocaine.html).

This site will help both you and your loved ones understand what you are experiencing, as well as suggest other valuable resources for you to consider. The latest treatment studies will be available to you in a simplified, easy to apply manner.

20| Multiple Addictions: How to Cope

Addiction is a disease that manifests itself in numerous ways. Many people with the disease of addiction struggle with multiple addictive "crutches." For instance, most people who have an addiction to crack/cocaine also have an addiction to alcohol. Many times the "primary" addiction, as it is referred to, seems to be the only one causing the user trouble at the time. However, one very common occurrence is that crack/cocaine abusers will stop using and find themselves drinking excessively or using heroin as a downer. Additionally, the "process" addictions (which are more components of the compulsive nature of the disease), such as gambling, work and sex will also simultaneously manifest themselves within the user.

While it's impossible to rid yourself of every addictive tendency when you cease crack/cocaine use, it is HIGHLY recommended that you cease use of all mind-altering substances (other than those prescribed and monitored by a doctor) when you decide to recover from a crack/cocaine addiction. If you don't, there is a strong likelihood that you will find yourself starting your recovery process all over again a year or two or 20 later.

21| Marijuana Facts and Patterns

According to the website for the National Institute on Drug Abuse, marijuana is the most commonly abused illicit drug in the United States. It is a common part of addiction recovery lexicon to refer to marijuana as the "gateway drug." Most people who indulge in regular marijuana use end up abusing other, often more dangerous drugs, such as heroin, crack, cocaine and, of course, alcohol.

Marijuana negatively affects the brain, heart, lungs and, often the entire immune system. Depression and even anxiety are prevalent with use. If you feel that you have a problem with marijuana, you should attempt cease use immediately. If you suffer symptoms, such as inability to sleep, heightened anxiety/irritability, or even increased feelings of aggression, you should consult a doctor immediately. For further information log onto www.nida.gov (from here, other resources will be easy to retrieve).

22| Medical/Psychological Support for Recovery from Marijuana Addiction

Many people suffer from biochemical stressors such as anxiety, depression or insecurity prior to indulgence of marijuana. This drug is often taken in higher and higher doses to self-medicate such symptoms. Unfortunately, while use may temporarily alleviate discomfort, prolonged use (and the eventual need to withdraw/detox) only exacerbate the problem.

If you suffer from persistent anxiety and/or depression, it is likely that these symptoms will worsen upon marijuana withdrawal and/or cessation. It is recommended that you avoid attempting to self-medicate in other ways (such as turning to alcohol, heroin, sex or overeating) to cope with your anxiety. It is also suggested that you recognize your need for medical attention and that you seek help from both a psychiatrist and a therapist who are experienced in the area(s) of addiction.

Psychiatrists differ from therapists in that they are trained to focus on the chemical components of the addiction and necessary treatment of pre-existing symptoms. The therapist will help you cope with the inevitable feelings and emotions you will experience as a result of use cessation. In order to receive maximum benefits from these services, it is necessary that you be honest about your addiction and history of use and that you take recommended suggestions from your doctors. In order to find the best doctor/therapist to suit your recovery needs, you should consult with a trusted medical doctor.

23| Physical Effects of Withdrawal from Marijuana Abuse

As stated previously, the psychological effects of marijuana use cessation are numerous. Again, these include insomnia, irritability, anxiety and even unexplainable anger/rage. Physical symptoms of withdrawal can also be debilitating. Common physical manifestations of withdrawal are headaches, eating problems (early loss of appetite and/or cramping), and heavy sweating. These symptoms are common physiological responses to bombarding one's body with toxins. And, yes, excessive marijuana consumption would be considered toxic to the body.

It is suggested that in order to cope with such symptoms, you drink a lot of water, lay off the caffeine (which will only enhance insomnia) and stay away from too much fatty food. Additionally, practice some new self-care behaviors that you would offer anyone with a severe case of the flu: eat chicken soup, take a bath, relax and read a book, and get some rest.

24| Individualized Drug Counseling

It has been researched that drug addicts who add individualized drug counseling as a part of their drug rehab program are more successful than recovering addicts who merely cease use. The role of the drug counselor is to help you deal with the emotional and environmental consequences of your disease. For example, he she will help you deal with such things as how to address your addiction in the workplace (or how to deal with being out of work), housing assistance, and education on negative repetitive thought/behavioral patterns. This person will be both non-judgmental and well-educated on the distorted thought processes of your addiction.

A good place to find Certified Alcohol and Drug Counselors (CADCs) is through local mental health centers or hospitals. If these venues do not have their own drug counselors in house, they will have social workers who can offer you case management/referral services to get the help you need.

25| Marijuana Anonymous as a Form of Relapse Prevention

Marijuana Anonymous is a 12-step recovery program (an offshoot of Alcoholics Anonymous) where men/women who have a desire to cease abusive use of marijuana come together for support. The website, Marijuana-anonymous.org, is highly recommended for you to peruse if you think you may have a problem with marijuana. Particularly helpful are the "twelve questions" to help you determine if you do in fact have a problem and the international meeting directory.

If you do decide that attendance at an MA meeting would be useful to you, this site also has such useful information as what you can expect when you attend a meeting (because those early days can be very scary) and recommended literature to get you started.

26| Alternatives to Marijuana Anonymous

Since Marijuana Anonymous is a fairly new fellowship, it tends to be harder to find as a resource, particularly in smaller cities. Even major cities tend to only have about two meetings per week. This minimal amount of support, while beneficial, will not be sufficient to ensure your long-term sobriety. Some other suggestions are as follows:

- If you have computer access on a regular basis, MA offers one online meeting each day. See Marijuana-Anonymous.org for details
- Narcotics Anonymous is a bit larger as a fellowship and is easier to find. Since you are a marijuana smoker, you most likely have used/abused various other chemicals as well. Go to www.na.org for further details.
- Alcoholics Anonymous is the first of the twelve-step fellowship, the most established, and the easiest to find. All other twelve-step programs are based on the philosophy of this original one. It is suggested that you first attend open AA meetings to meet people with a similar problem to you.

Another note: If you are trying to cease marijuana use, the general belief is that all substance use must cease. Even if alcohol isn't your "primary" addiction, it is most likely something that is coupled with your marijuana use.

27| Learning More About Recovery From Drug Addiction

The National Institute on Drug Abuse website (nida.nih.gov) has an excellent and comprehensive list of points to consider when seeking treatment for any substance abuse problem. Marijuana is no exception. These "Principles of Drug Addiction Treatment" are a recommended starting place to give yourself a brief overview of what your recovery needs might be.

One important point to highlight here is that drug abuse is a chronic condition. It is important that you do not forget at any point in your recovery that marijuana addiction (as with all substance abuse) is considered a mental illness according to the *Diagnostic and Statistical Manual of Mental Disorders (IV)*. This means that, as with any mental illness, recovery will be a lifelong process with peaks and valleys and that your recovery needs will evolve and change over time.

28| Marijuana as a Secondary Addiction

If you have a problem with marijuana, chances are you have multiple other substance addictions. According to the United States Department of Health and Human Services more than 50 percent of those admitted to treatment for marijuana addiction (in 2000) did not report marijuana as their primary addiction.

If you are beginning your journey of recovery from marijuana addiction it is recommended that you also take a look at your alcohol usage, and use or abuse of any other substances. Many people feel that if they use marijuana more than they use alcohol, then they only have to cease use of marijuana. Although it may seem difficult to cease use (and seek support) for all substances that you are currently abusing, it may save your life.

29| Court Mandated Rehabilitation

If a judge mandates that you seek rehabilitation for marijuana or other drug addiction then you have no choice but to follow-through. If you are court mandated to partake in rehab, it is highly likely that you will be required to attend at least one twelve-step meeting per week for approximately six months. Upon attendance, you will be expected to have your court papers signed by the meeting moderator to prove attendance. Inpatient Treatment, Outpatient Treatment and even treatment modalities like anger-management classes and/or therapy may be required.

It is recommended that if you have been court mandated to seek support for your addiction that you do your best to keep an open mind and to embrace yourself in this opportunity for recovery. Chances are that if you got in trouble with the law because of your marijuana use, you are faced with a very serious addiction problem. If you do not take this mandated recovery opportunity as a learning experience, you will most likely use again and end up in the same exact place later.

30| Suggested Supplements to 12-Step Programs

Other supportive modalities, such as cognitive behavioral therapy, medication management, and even housing support (which can be sought through a case manager/social worker at a local hospital or agency with specialty in addiction recovery) can be beneficial therapies. It is sometimes recommended that an addict in early recovery live in a halfway house, a recovery home (which tends to be far more expensive) or with sober friends.

Early recovery from addiction should not include spending significant amounts of time with peers, or even family members who use drugs and alcohol. This behavior will almost always lead to relapse. Some of the people to expect to run into are certified drug and alcohol counselors (CADC), social workers, nurses, physicians and psychologists. The important thing to consider for the latter named professionals is their level of knowledge and experience dealing with your specific area of addiction difficulty.

31| Narcotic Addiction: Am I Addicted?

"Narcotics" is a broad term used to refer to many types of drugs. The most commonly abused narcotic is heroin. Despite the stereotype of a "street person" being addicted to heroin, many people who are addicted to narcotics become so when prescribed medicine for pain.

Drugs such as morphine, Percocet, and Dilauded initially relieve some very intense pain. Unfortunately, though, many people become addicted to either the euphoria or sedation that is stimulated in the central nervous system by such drugs. If you are taking narcotics for pain and think you may have a problem, it is essential that you pay attention to the symptoms that manifest themselves in your body over time. Some of these are numbness, chronic sedation, shallow breathing, constipation, persistent nausea and flushed skin. These symptoms are common signs of narcotic abuse.

Most importantly, if you feel increased dependence with decreased effects, mental obsession with when/how you will get to your narcotics and withdrawal symptoms upon use cessation, it would be a good idea to seek treatment immediately.

32| Narcotics and Other Drug Abuse

According to a 2002 report by the Drug Abuse Warning Network (DAWN) out of the U.S. Department of Health; oxycodone, alcohol, benzodiazepines, and cocaine are commonly used in conjunction with each other. This means that seeking treatment for the abuse of oxycodone or heroin does not mean that these are the only drugs you will need to give up. It is common in the recovery lexicon to refer to a particular substance as one's "drug of choice."

The vast majority of treatment plans, however, including those found in hospital settings, outpatient settings and in 12-step settings advocate complete cessation of all chemical substances in order to maintain a sober life. This may seem to be a tall order at first, but if you wish to lead a happy, healthier and more fulfilling life complete substance abstinence is highly suggested. If you don't give it all up now, you will quickly find that the insidious nature of the thinking and obsessive aspects of addiction will simply lead you to another primary substance to abuse.

33| Learning the Drug Recovery Lexicon

If you are interested in seeking treatment for narcotic abuse, or want to learn more about symptoms you may be experiencing, start with the basics. Just like in any field of work or even recovery, there are key terms with which one should become familiar prior to or during treatment. The reason for this recommendation is that recovery can be overwhelming and frightening on many levels.

Recovery is often the first time that drug addicts are asked to be honest about themselves and their behaviors over their period of use, so being somewhat comfortable with terms that will be thrown out can be helpful to increased feelings of safety and decreased feelings of shame (based on lack of awareness of the disease component of drug addiction).

eGetgoing is an excellent site that offers "Drug and Alcohol Information: Glossary" and outlines terms such as abstinence, 12-Steps, associated mental illnesses (like ADHD and Bipolar Disorder), detox, and tolerance.

34| Legal Narcotics

Narcotics, which are opiates, can be classified into either prescription (or legal) narcotics/drugs or street narcotics/drugs. It is important to note a common misconception regarding "legal" drugs, which is that they are always safe and/or non-addictive. This is not true. In fact, legal drugs, such as alcohol or prescription narcotics are among the most abused drugs (i.e. Codeine, Methadone, Morphine, Percodan, Vicodin, Percocet). While all are addictive, the latter three are particularly dependence forming. Tranquilizers, sedatives, certain muscle relaxants, prescription amphetamines, Oxycotin over the counter drugs (i.e. mouthwashes and diet aids) can also be addictive.

It is important to note that if you are someone who struggles with a history of addiction of any kind, that you tell your health care provider this prior to being prescribed any of the above substances. And even if you are not an addict currently, it is recommended that you really weigh the costs and benefits of taking certain medications. There are many people who become addicts due to chronic pain and increased dependency on chemical substances for physical relief. Narcotics can be very helpful in reducing intolerable pain/discomfort, but, again, be certain that your motivations for use are "clean" and that you are open and honest with your doctor regarding use patterns and physical need.

35| Community Reinforcement as a Form of Rehabilitation

There are numerous types of recovery approaches. One such method is titled the Community Reinforcement model. Simply put, this model promotes a variety of recovery activities that will lead to an overall change in thinking, behavior and support development. Research proves that combining a variety of treatments, such as individual/group therapy, medication (when necessary), case management support, and membership in some self-help group (Narcotics Anonymous, Alcoholics Anonymous, Rational Recovery) ensures the most effective treatment outcomes over time. Those who engage in all aspects of the recovery mix (such as those mentioned above) are the most successful in achieving long-term and fulfilling sobriety. Statistics support this experience. The rationale here is that one's thinking, behavioral and experiential practices have proven unsuccessful and that a support network will be essential in order to make an overall lifestyle and behavioral change.

36| Heroin Detox: The Methadone Question

As with any form of detox, it is essential that you check yourself into a detoxification program where your body will have time to safely heal from the physiological dependency it has acquired on heroin. Heroin detox generally lasts between 7-14 days.

The next step is deciding whether or not you plan to engage in methadone management. One opinion is that methadone management is not a treatment regiment that promotes total and long-term sobriety. That being said, however, since the risk of relapse and possible death are highest right after initial detox, methadone can help some people early on. Although methadone produces a different and more time-released high, some people become dependent on the methadone as well.

The addictive mind and body are generally looking for any "out" from discomfort. Methadone can be a tricky and dangerous way to try to treat a brain that is already addicted/dependent upon a chemical substance to function. That being said, it is always recommended that you do your own research. Go to the library, go to 12-step meetings, talk with the medical professionals at your detox center and speak with both professionals and other addicts who can give you information based on their clinical and personal experiences.

37| Opiate Detox Options

Opiate detox procedures have been a misunderstood, controversial and slowly evolving animal. Clinically speaking, it is suggested that those seeking help for opiate detox do a good deal of "homework" prior to selecting which program works. (***Note***: If you are in an urgent situation in terms of need for detox help, then it is most important that you check yourself into the nearest hospital detox program because detoxing alone is a very dangerous decision and one that, because of the intense discomfort, leads to relapse).

You have several opiate detox program options to consider. Traditional detox procedures involve checking into a medical facility where specialists are able to monitor chemical levels and withdrawal symptoms. Detox, however, does not end after initial withdrawal. This kind of procedure lasts a very long time (the thinking, in general, is that it takes at least 18 months to completely rid your system of the substances). While this is a grueling way to detox, it does follow the thinking that there is no quick fix to recovery (and many addicts are seeking a quick fix mentality) and that the changing process must last a lifetime.

Rapid Detox, simply put, is a more neophyte detox method (about 10 years in the making) that suggests opiate detox can be accomplished without adverse affects in a very short time. Caution is urged prior to embarking on any quick-fix procedure. It is recommended that you speak with other recovering people prior to making a decision on what will work for you.

38| Self-Help/12-Step Groups as Part of Recovery

Recovering from drug addiction is a grueling, often difficult and ultimately rewarding process. While the research regarding 12-step program success rates is limited, often due to the anonymity principle indicated in such programs, clinical evidence shows that the overall success rates are very high-given a willingness to practice new behaviors and an authentic desire to receive help.

Getting sober is the most difficult decision a person may every make, as it is a willingness to let go of the only "support network" you have come to know. Chances are that you have lost or are beginning to lose friends, jobs, family and, more importantly self-respect. This doesn't get better over time, only far worse. The reason 12-step programs appear to be successful is because they offer a network of support where you will not find judgment for your mistakes/losses, but understanding. Additionally, you will find people who will hold you accountable for your past behaviors and current behaviors, while continuing to treat you with respect. From a clinical perspective, such cohesiveness and installation of hope do give people the desire/openness to change. That being said, 12-step programs do require action (not money, though) on the part of the recovering person. You must do something different in order to get different results. It is suggested that you pick up a copy of both the traditional Alcoholics Anonymous text (*The Big Book of Alcoholics Anonymous*) and the Narcotics Anonymous text (which was derived from the original). If you identify with any of the stories, suggestions in this book, then you will most likely benefit from 12-step programs.

39| Street Narcotics

Street narcotics are becoming increasingly popular among teenagers and adults in recent years. Common street narcotics include ecstasy, cocaine, hallucinogens (psychedelic drugs), crack cocaine, amphetamines, Rohypnol, steroids, inhalants and solvents, ketamine, heroin, marijuana, phencyclidine (PCP) and methadone. While these individual drugs types will be further explored in individual categories, they are important to note as a family/class of drugs. Many of these "street" narcotics are used in concordance with one another.

As previously stated, marijuana is known as the "gateway drug," which can lead to use of more addictive drugs, such as cocaine and heroin. Most people who indulge in drug use do not limit themselves to one type of drug. Often times, one starts off with alcohol or marijuana, and needs increasing amounts of energy (cocaine), then downers (heroin) and so on. The cycle becomes worse and more intense until none of the sensations are achieving the level of satisfaction for the user that was originally experienced. It is during this time that the user begins to lose important people and things in life, go to jail, or even experience near-death experiences or real death. The alternative is to get help.

40| Withdrawal From Narcotics

Common withdrawal signs are irritability, salivation, intense cravings for your drug of choice, decreased appetite, diarrhea, vomiting and muscle aches. As with any other drug, the more you use and the longer you've used the more severe the withdrawal symptoms.

It is recommended that if you plan to detox from any narcotics from which you experience withdrawal you check yourself into an inpatient medical facility where the staff is trained in drug withdrawal.

41| Pain Killer Overview

"Pain killers" is a term used to refer to prescription narcotics that are used to treat chronic and/or severe pain. Pain killers are similar to alcohol in that they repress the user's central nervous system. Some examples of pain killers commonly prescribed are Codeine, Methadone, Morphine, Percodan, Vicodin and Percocet. These kinds of medications can be prescribed for anything from severe back pain to a bad case of shingles to cancer. The major problem with the frequent distribution and use of pain killers, however, is that they are highly addictive substances and can often lead people with non-addictive pasts to acquire addictive tendencies. If you are in chronic pain, but have a history of addictive substance use, it is highly recommended that you notify your primary health care physician and/or specialist prior to being prescribed any of the above. That way you can make an informed decision about the possible side effects of use, as well as receive information about any alternative forms of medication/treatment to alleviate pain. At the very least, it is crucial for anyone taking pain killers to have their intake monitored with scrutiny by the distributing physician.

42| Pain Killer Addiction

Pain killer addiction, while still a severe problem, tends to be researched or discussed less frequently than addiction(s) to alcohol and other "street" drugs. Pain killers are often used to treat persons who have been unexpectedly overcome with severe pain and who require some alleviation of this pain for normal or even functional living. Just because these drugs are administered "legally," however, the addiction problem can be just as severe and life threatening as addiction to any other chemical substance. And just like one becomes physiologically and mentally dependent on alcohol and heroin, the same occurs when one experiences addiction to pain killers. The problem with pain killers is twofold: they are legally distributed to several million Americans each year and they are very addictive by nature. Such common pain killers as Vicodin and even Oxycotin have become among numerous prescription narcotics to adversely affect otherwise non-drug using men and women. While the use, as already stated, generally starts as a response to an unplanned and uncontrolled stimulus (pain, in this case), the addiction then manifests as a chemical dependency over time. At this point, more and more amounts of the pain killer(s) are taken to alleviate pain. And in some cases, the pain can become psychosomatic, just so that the now addicted person can find an "excuse" to continue or justify indulgence.

43| Chronic Pain vs. Pain Killer Consumption

While pain killers have increased in terms of an addictive problem over recent years, the number of overall cases of men and women addicted to pain killers is still relatively small compared to other substances (like alcohol, for example). If you are in chronic pain, the reality is that the pain can also lead to major depression and even substance abuse of another kind. It is not uncommon for those suffering chronic pain to become addicted to alcohol or other related substances when they are not treated. The recommendation is that if you are in chronic pain, but frightened that you will become addicted to pain killers:

- Research pain killer addiction (trends) online and at the library and determine the pros and cons related to your situation
- Talk to your doctor/therapist openly and be honest about your pain and motivation for taking the medication
- If you are already in a 12-step program, don't hide your desire from your sponsor (this may be a sign of addictive motivations), but be proactive in stating that you are seeking medical/expert advice.
- If you still do not feel comfortable taking pain killers, then seek out alternative forms of medication (i.e., naturopath, chiropractic, acupuncture).
- If you are in recovery, you did not go there to be in chronic pain. You can find help without having to suffer through severe physical torture.

44| Oxycotin Detox: Methadone Maintenance

One of the treatment modalities for detox from heroin abuse is methadone maintenance. This use as part of the recovery process has proven very controversial over the years. Since Oxycotin, a commonly prescribed and abused pain killer, has very similar affects on the body to heroin, methadone maintenance programs have become a more popular form of treatment for Oxycotin detox. Professionally speaking, it is generally the thinking that without total abstinence from use, one does not recover from drug addiction over the long term. While methadone maintenance can certainly make the process of withdrawal less traumatic over the short term, methadone use can easily lead to another chemical dependency and, yet, another need for treatment over time. Addiction and addict thinking are inherently "impatient." Addicts become dependent on a quick fix both chemically and emotionally. The problem - from a clinical perspective - with feeding into this quick fix mentality, is that the addict thinking and behavioral manifestations, then, are not adequately addressed, and the addictive tendencies, thus, permeate the user for the long term. While short-term detox, coupled with behavioral therapy and some form of 12-step treatment take a lot of effort and time, the results tend to be more fruitful and successful over the long run.

45| Oxycotin Addiction

Ever since the media stories about Rush Limbaugh's demise from Oxycotin addiction, Americans have been more aware of this commonly prescribed pain killer. Oxycotin, as with all pain killers, is in the opioid family, and is often described as "prescription heroin." All opioids have a "downer" affect and, thus, pain killers not only alleviate the "pain," but also make the user quite relaxed and even laid back. The problem with drugs like Oxycotin is that once the "low euphoria" wears off, the pain and the stress related to both pain and other parts of life return. These normal feelings of anxiety, fear and stress become less tolerable to the user and he/she begins to seek a quick fix for comfort once again. It is not uncommon for men and women who develop Oxycotin addiction to begin to seek out other drugs, such as alcohol, to enhance the feelings of contentment and/or relaxation they seek. One sure sign of addiction to Oxycotin, or any pain killer for that matter, is when the user begins to realize that he/she can no longer obtain the desired medication from his/her doctor and begins to seek out illegal drugs, or street pain killers. If he/she cannot obtain illegal pain killers, this may lead the now addicted user to seek out drugs like heroin to achieve a similar high.

46| Pain Killer Dependency: Risk of Addiction

While pain killer addiction is a real and recurring problem, it should be noted that there are some high risk factors that may indicate more susceptibility to addictive tendencies:

- Those with a history of substance abuse (related to anything from alcohol, heroin, marijuana) are far more likely to develop an addiction to pain killers when prescribed. The reason for this is that the addictive thought and biochemical processes have already been triggered. The thinking here is that once one's body has been altered by chemical dependency/addiction, he/she will return to those processes once any addictive substance is consumed.
- Family history of substance abuse
- Recent history of psychological and/or emotional problems that may lead to desire to "escape" feelings.

This being said, it is important to note that no one should determine your need for pain killers other than you and your medical doctor. It is crucial that you look at your history of use and abuse, as well as your motivations for consumption, and be perfectly open and honest with your health care team prior to consumption.

47| Pain Killer Addiction Process

Many people are confused by the fact that pain killers, which are often initially prescribed to alleviate discomfort or pain, can become addictive to the body. The most commonly addictive pain killers are the opioids (like morphine, codeine). To give you an idea of how addictive opioids are, heroin is a street drug version of an opioid. While these pain killers do work to change the way that the body responds to pain, they also begin to achieve a feeling of lightness and/or euphoria in the user. If a person becomes attached to this euphoria (not hard to do with a body full of a pain and a life full of stress), then he/she will begin to take the medication over a long period of time and even begin to deny to him/herself that this is not the proper use of the medication. After prolonged use of pain killers, the body chemistry is altered and a physiological dependency develops to the particular pain killer(s) being consumed. Once the body chemistry is altered, the person becomes in danger of major symptoms of physical and emotional withdrawal and in need of a reputable detox and recovery program.

48| Pain Killer Withdrawal

One problem with men and women who are not closely monitored in their use of pain killers (which generally occurs as part of the addiction cycle) are withdrawal symptoms that can be both uncomfortable and dangerous. Common symptoms of withdrawal from pain killers are:

- restlessness
- bone pain
- muscle pain
- cold flashes
- vomiting
- diarrhea
- muscle spasms

If you think that you may have a problem with pain killer addiction, it is highly recommended that you do not try and withdraw in a "cold turkey" fashion. There are numerous medical and treatment facilities where you can detox safely, and under the care of qualified professionals, and receive connections and/or referrals to reputable treatment programs.

49| Pain Killer Rehab: Short-Term Recovery Plan

Another rehabilitation approach goes with the understanding that most pain killer addicts did not initially indulge in drugs to behave defiantly and/or get high, but to alleviate pain. This approach uses an intense focus on physical detox, along with individual therapy and a short-term, intensive treatment. This type of rehab program does not tend to emphasize the importance of total abstinence over the long term. Clinically speaking, it is often the case that someone who becomes addicted to pain killers becomes co-addicted to at least one other substance (alcohol is a good example). In the rare case that this does not occur, the above stated rehabilitation plan may prove successful. It must be noted, however, that addictive tendencies and behaviors can forever alter a person's chemical and thought-processes. If this is the case, a short rehab stint may not prove successful.

50| Pain Killer Rehab: Total Abstinence

Rehabilitation for pain killers is approached in several different ways. While some recovering addicts, as well as professionals in the field, view pain killer addiction as indistinct from any other chemical dependency, others disagree. Here we will focus on the camp that feels that total abstinence of all substances is necessary to achieve real recovery. This side of the recovery world feels that a short-term detoxification program should be coupled with a lifelong 12-step program. Individual and/or group therapy is often utilized in this treatment approach. If this sort of recovery option seems "over the top" to you, be careful not to jump to early conclusions.

The decision to embark on this kind of recovery program may be the most fruitful, especially if the pain killer addict in question was using any other substances simultaneously, or was using pain killers as an additional substance after already exhibiting a problem with multiple substances. While it is sometimes the case that patients who have no history of chemical dependency are innocently prescribed pain killers and get a bad deal out of it, this is not always the case. Most long-term, hard core addicts use multiple substances. Even if pain killers are the "drug of choice," this does not mean that cessation of only that group of drugs will lead to a sober life. In fact, it is likely that another drug will creep up as the addict culprit as soon as the use of pain killers is aborted.

51| Drug Relapse Statistics/Trends

According to the educational text *Substance Abuse Counseling: Theory and Practice* (2005), "Some believe that the 'most common treatment outcome for alcoholics and addicts is relapse.'" (291; Dimeff & Marlatt, 1995, p. 176). This fact remains true, even 12 years after this quote was initially published. According to AA, relapse involves the resuming of pre-recovery use and behaviors and the need to start again from the beginning of the recovery process. Even if you have 29 years sober, if you relapse, you are back at square one and step one. And sometimes, people who relapse never get another chance to recover. A "dry" addict or alcoholic is someone who simply ceases use, but does not embark on any of the mental, physical and even spiritual changes that are suggested for an optimal life experience. A "recovering" addict is someone who not only ceases use, but who works hard to change his/her history of distorted thinking and self-destructive behaviors, and seeks a network of support through which he/she can give and receive assistance. It is strongly suggested that you be aware of the following sure signs of potential relapse during your recovery:

- Getting involved in other compulsive/impulsive behaviors or addictions (i.e. eating too much, sleeping around, shopping constantly, or even becoming obsessed with AA).

- Being unaware of your feelings/needs and/or not meeting your basic needs. It is important to eat, sleep, rest and have play time in-between work and recovery time.
- Closed mindedness or a refusal to try a new way of viewing the world.
- Continuing to hang around the same people and embark on the same journeys and expect things to turn out differently.

52| Early Relapse Prevention: Avoiding Major Life Changes When Possible

One of the common features of alcoholic/addict behavior is the tendency to seek impulsive and often self-defeating highs. This tendency can manifest itself in more than just drug/alcohol use. The first year of sobriety can often be more painful than the fun (or even painful) days of using, because the alcoholic/addict is so used to numbing and avoiding painful feelings. If a person is really focusing on his/her recovery, those painful feelings will soon come to the surface. The tendency is for the person in early recovery to medicate these feelings by causing chaos or excitement in other areas of his/her life. Major geographic, job, relationship, financial, or lifestyle changes are highly discouraged in the first months and year of recovery. This suggestion is very hard for a person in early sobriety to grasp, as he/she is accustomed and even programmed to do something to escape feelings. Note: For unavoidable changes, like getting fired, a partner leaving you, losing your home, death of a loved one, it is essential that you seek the support of other sober friends, a sponsor and possibly a mental health professional to cope with your situation and to avoid relapse.

53| Know Your Triggers for Drug/Alcohol Use

A "trigger" is something that prompts one to think about, crave, and ultimately relapse on drugs/alcohol. Triggers vary depending on the alcoholic/addict and his/her history and patterns of use. For example, some alcoholics cannot go to bars after they get sober (at least for a long time), because it makes them think about the "romantic" aspects of their use. Others are fine in bars, because they always drank alone in their apartments. Other common triggers for use are sex (or unhealthy emotional entanglements), other addictions to things like shopping, food, and work, or being in touch with former using friends. While each addict has much in common, each addict has differing patterns of use. It is suggested that you make a list of your past use "triggers" and be sure to avoid them at all costs. If you need to be in a particular situation (and as the *Big Book of AA* says, "if you have a legitimate reason for being there") then check with sober friends and/or a sponsor to get suggestions for coping. It is also recommended that those of you in your first year of sobriety read the book *Living Sober: Some Methods AA Members Have Used for Not Drinking*, as it has a lot of details and suggestions regarding common trigger situations and alternative coping skills (other than alcohol/drug abuse)

54| How to Pick a Sponsor

One of the major components of ay 12-step program is the presence of a "sponsor." The sponsor is the person who essentially looks after the person in recovery and helps him/her work their 12 steps. Before choosing a sponsor, it is suggested that you go to various meetings (especially early on) and listen and watch the members there. If you like what someone has to say (or think you'd like the recovery they seem to have), then get to know him/her a bit better. Ask that person to coffee and find out what you have in common, and find out his/her focus in the 12-step program. Additionally, it is suggested that you work with someone who has worked through the 12 steps already.

55| Finding a Spiritual Connection to Avoid Relapse

Some people have a difficult time grasping the concept of a "Higher Power" suggested in 12-Step programs. The good news is that there is no spiritual or religious requirement for membership in such a group. The only requirement is your desire to stop using drugs and/or alcohol. Anything else is something that each person tailors to meet his/her needs. It is suggested that one find some sort of spiritual connection in maintaining sobriety. It can be a tree, a shoe, a crab-cake, or a good orderly direction (note the usage G.O.D. as an acronym).

56| Obtaining a Network of Recovery Support

One of the hallmark behaviors of people who relapse is failure to obtain a network of support. The addicts tendency is to isolate, withdraw and to be convinced that he/she "has this taken care of on my own." That is an automatic prescription for relapse, because the addict thought processes are constantly searching for a way to make you drink, drug, and ultimately die. For this reason, it is crucial that you connect with both program members and non-program members (for example, a sister or friend who does not have a drinking problem, but whom is very supportive of your seeking help) so that you have healthy people (and healthy thoughts) surrounding you. Be honest with the people you trust about your efforts and verbalize your need for their support. This practice will feel awkward at first, but you will be surprised how many people really care about you and want you to be well.

57| Professional Help in Relapse Prevention

Many people attempting to get sober have long struggled with other forms of mental illness. Such manifestations can range from mild, ongoing depression to Generalized Anxiety Disorder, to extreme cases of Paranoid Schizophrenia. These are serious forms of mental illness and cannot be treated individually or even with a 12-step treatment alone. It is suggested that you seek the support of a psychiatrist and/or a therapist (note: most psychiatrists are excellent at medication management, but not therapy, so a separate counselor is suggested if it is within your budget). Most cities have local mental health centers that offer discounted rates for such services. If you do opt to seek professional help, however, it is essential that you tell your provider(s) that you are a recovering alcoholic. This way, you will not be prescribed any other drugs to which you can become addicted. Note: If you find a sponsor or group of 12-step members who tell you that you cannot have a therapist or take medication, think again. This sect of the recovery program is not supported by the World Service Office of Alcoholics Anonymous. Twelve-step programs are self-help groups, not a group of medical professionals. If seeing a doctor makes you nervous, there are plenty of recovering psychiatrists/therapists that you can find through networking in your program.

58| Twelve-Step Meetings as a Part of Relapse Prevention

A major factor in obtaining long-term sobriety (from any drug or alcohol) is membership in a 12-Step Program. If your drug of choice is crack/cocaine, it is suggested that you attend Cocaine Anonymous (when available to you), coupled with Alcoholics Anonymous (for a larger and stronger network of support). These programs work because you are surrounded with an instant network of people who understand the exact feelings, thoughts and behaviors you have, are and will experience. It is suggested that you attend a variety of meetings in your area so that you can find a group or several groups that work for you. A home group (which means a group that you attend every week at the same time) is suggested, so that accountability and consistent support can be accomplished. To find a list of meetings in your area to alcoholics-anonymous.org

59| Recovery Choices Outside of Twelve-Step Programming

It is my repeated clinical experience that the most effective way for anyone to recover from addiction/alcoholism is through 12-step programs. That being said, I also believe in presenting my clients with a variety of options. Excellent resources to couple with 12-step programs are residential treatment (especially for those with a history of relapse), sober halfway house living, intensive outpatient therapy, and even inpatient treatment for those in the very first stages of recovery. Other treatment modalities, such as harm-reduction (most often used in treatment of the chronically mentally ill), rational recovery, social skills training, or cognitive behavioral therapy (to name a few) are also options to consider. More information on these can be obtained both online and at any larger library. It is important for you to do the research yourself, talk to people with similar experiences, and decide what form of treatment can help you lead a happy, healthy and drug/alcohol free life!

60| Relapse Prevention: Have a Plan

One of the inevitable aspects of lifelong recovery from alcohol/drug abuse is that you will have cravings from time-to-time. The average craving only lasts about 60 seconds. It is the indulgence in the thought or the possibility of use that makes a negative thought or craving last for days on end. It is important that you have a plan in place for such moments. Here are some plan-in-place ideas:

- Have several support people on speed dial. This way, if one isn't available when you call, you can call someone else, and you don't have to take the time to find any numbers.
- Stand Still. If you are standing in the middle of the street, you can't do anything silly (like drink or use).
- Just start running. Even in place. Again, this may sound silly, but you can run this thought off by focusing on something else.
- Have a round the clock list of meetings on hand. Go to one immediately if you can.
- Do the dishes.
- BREATHE through the feeling

61| Alcohol Statistics

It is estimated that deaths related to alcohol consumption (liver failure, strokes, driving) reach about 100,000 people per year. To put this into perspective, it is also estimated that in 2002 over 16,000 people died from all drug overdoses combined. In other words, although alcohol is a legal drug, it is far more accessible and even more dangerous to the body over a long period of time (it should also be considered that those abusing drugs are usually drinking in conjunction with their drug use). A frightening statistic, according to Mothers Against Drunk Driving, is that alcohol consumption/abuse is responsible for the death(s) of 6.5 times more teenagers than all other combined drugs. Also, even though drinking socially is a common occurrence, about 18 percent of the population will eventually struggle with an alcohol abuse problem. These statistics may seem high, and that is because the alcohol related, societal and health problems are quite severe. So don't be fooled by a fancy label or a beautiful woman sipping a chardonnay. The realities can certainly be less romantic.

62| Drug Overdose/Poisoning

Illegal drug overdose, while a significant problem, does not kill nearly as many people per year as alcohol abuse and misuse. That being said, however, the statistics regarding drug-related deaths are stark. According to *Medical News Today*, there was a marked increase between the number of drug related deaths between 1979 and 1990 (5.3% per year) and between 1990 and 2002 (18.1% per year). Interestingly, the majority of these deaths are reported as being related to opioid-type pain killers (it should be noted, however, that it may be more "acceptable" to report pain killers on a death certificate than heroin consumption, so the research will be affected by such lack of control). Regardless of any deviances in research, these facts certainly highlight that drug abuse is a serious problem. The truth is, the easier drugs are to obtain, the easier they are to abuse.

63| Inhalant Statistics

Inhalants can refer to the use of chemical substances, such as aerosols, gasses, and cleaning agents to get high. While inhalants are not as widely researched and discussed as other drugs, they are indicated as a serious problem related to teenage, drug-related deaths. Sudden Sniffing Death Syndrome, which accounts for over 50% of inhalant related deaths, can affect the user even upon the first attempt to inhale. In fact, according to drug statistics on *In the Know Zone*, 22% of people who died from inhalant related SSDS were first time users. Suffocation and vomit in the lungs are two other contributors to death by inhalant use. Inhalants are a popular way to "get high" among teenagers, aged 13-17.

64| Juveniles and Drugs

There are several relevant risk factors that can determine the possibility of drug use/abuse for juveniles:

- genetic predisposition
- stressful environment
- peer pressure
- mental illness and desire to self-medicate

It should be noted that the earlier the onset of drug use/abuse, the more likely that the user will develop increased drug problems over his/her life. This pattern of use becomes not only a part of the juvenile's formative physiological and chemical make-up, but also an early integrated, albeit defective, coping strategy. While reports of drug use/abuse regarding juveniles show a recent decline in overall use, the concern with juvenile use patterns (and related behavioral and societal difficulties) is being addressed on a national level. A 2006 *Monitoring the Future* study reported that 36.5 % of 12th graders reported use within the last year. 21.5% of that same group reported use over the past month. Other research reports that engagement in relational, youth activities appears to decrease the overall tendency of abuse patterns among juveniles.

65| Marijuana Use Patterns

Marijuana is often referred to as the "gateway drug," indicating that use of marijuana can easily lead to exploration of and even addiction to more potent and even more dangerous substances. For that reason, it is not surprising that according to the 2005 report by *The National Survey on Drug Use and Health*, 97.5 million Americans (12 and older) used the substance at least once. It is important here to acknowledge the term "at least;" this only means one use per lifetime at a minimum. In terms of prevalence of use of marijuana relative to those who were incarcerated in state and federal prisons between 1997 and 2004, the numbers are stark. Seventy-seven percent of state prisoners reported some use of marijuana prior to incarceration, as did 71.2 % of federal prisoners. These high percentages support the studies that show marijuana as a drug that leads to use of other substances. It should also be considered when reviewing these statistics that more people may be likely to report marijuana use, as it is more "acceptable" than use of drugs like heroin and/or cocaine.

66| Use Patterns of Cocaine

Cocaine use patterns have been documented by the National Survey of Drug Use and Health. According to a 2005 report, approximately 33.7 million Americans (aged 12 and beyond) had tried cocaine in their lifetime. More stark are the figures relative to tendency towards state or federal incarceration and tendency towards use over a lifetime. According to the same 2005 report, which surveyed former and current prisoners (incarcerated between 1997 and 2004) 46.8 % (state offenders) and 43.3% (federal offenders) of these criminals had reported some history of cocaine use. It is important to remember that with the above (and any) statistics, data is limited by both individual willingness to report and research design. In an interview conducted with several social workers who counsel former convicts, it was found that of approximately 60-80 clients each, close to 95% of these clients had reported use of cocaine over their lifetime(s).

67| Use Patterns of Ecstasy

Ecstasy can also be referred to as "X," "Adam" or "the love drug," and is frequently used in club settings to achieve a "free" or "uninhibited" state. Not unlike that good old "gateway" drug marijuana, those who use ecstasy are more likely to use and abuse other illicit drugs. Ecstasy also tends to be popular among teen populations. One frightening statistic, according to Partnership for a Drug-Free America, is that emergency visits linked to ecstasy use increased by approximately 2000 percent between 1994 and 2002. It's also reported that ecstasy tends to be the least popular drug discussed between parents and their kids. Death statistics related to ecstasy tend to be reported at lower rates. According to the 2000 *National Household Survey on Drug Abuse Statistics* by SAMHSA, deaths related to sole use of ecstasy were approximately 60 people out of 3,000,000 reported users. It must be noted, however, that if users were mixing multiple drugs, it may be difficult to determine the drug (or combination of) that was the direct cause of death.

68| Use Patterns of Heroin

Heroin is a member of the opioid family and considered the most addictive and widely used member of the bunch. Heroin is often injected, but can also be snorted or smoked. According to statistics researched and provided by *In the Know Zone*, between 1993 and 1999 the number of heroin users that reported past-month use almost tripled. Additionally, it was found that as of 2001, the number of emergency visits that had some relationship to heroin use was up to 14%. Another interesting statistic is that even though it is estimated that over 80% of heroin users use with another person, over 80% of those same users are found alone upon death. Interestingly, according to the 2005 study for *National Survey on Drug Use and Health*, more Americans (over age 12) report at least one use of heroin over a lifetime (3.5 million). Interestingly, however, the prevalence of heroin use reported over a lifetime in cases of state and federal incarceration is far lower than use reported in the same study regarding cocaine. Use at least once in a lifetime for these groups was reported at 23.4 % (state prisoners) and 17.9 % (federal).

69| Use Patterns Related to Nicotine

One would be remiss to provide a series of tips related to drug use/abuse statistics and not mention both the rampant use of and the detrimental effects of nicotine use and abuse. Whether you use/abuse alcohol and other drugs or not, nicotine statistics offer a stark perspective. People often disregard the outrageous danger of illness and death related to cigarette smoking. The U.S. Center for Disease Control estimates that approximately 100,000 Americans die per year related to alcohol abuse (relative to about 200 million reported drinkers), but that out of 100 million smokers, there are approximately 400,000 deaths. According to Terry Martin's *Global Smoking Statistics* for 2002, the "prognosis" for smokers looks grim. The estimate is that if smoking trends do not change, that 2030 will see the death of one in six people to smoking related illnesses.

70| Women and Drugs

While drug abuse was once considered a "man disease," the research regarding women and addiction is gaining prevalence. The National Center on Addiction and Substance Abuse at Columbia University conducted a 2005 study on young women and drug use. It was found that women aged eight to 22 years old abuse drugs for reasons different than men. The differences are not clearly indicated, but it may also be that women find that different reasons are more "socially acceptable" to report, because of the stigma not only related to substance abuse, but to women and abuse in particular. A 2004 report of nationwide admissions into drug treatment facilities showed that women made up 31.5% of this population. The important thing to note here is that the percentage is not only high, but it also only accounts for the women who actually admitted themselves (or were court mandated) for treatment. There are numerous mothers, housewives and very successful women whom suffer silently because they do not understand and/or believe that women can or do have substance abuse problems. It is possible, then, that women are less likely to report difficulties and/or less likely to receive treatment for substance related difficulties. The studies regarding drug type related to female abuse show similar trends to the drugs reported in overall population categories. Just as more people overall tend to use (or report use of) marijuana, more women reported use of marijuana on a regular basis than of consumption of other drugs. Drug use is also positively correlated with female incarceration. The Bureau of Justice Statistics reports that 59.3% of state female prisoners and 47.6% of federal female prisoners reported use within the month of arrest (2004).

71| Resources for Drug Rehabilitation Treatment

The choices regarding addiction rehabilitation are so numerous that it would require several books worth of information to provide adequate detail for an incoming, recovering addict. One very helpful resource in finding a treatment program that focuses on your individual needs is Drug Rehabs at 1-866 Sober12. This resource offers information relative to particular addictions (including process addictions like gambling and eating), state and type of facility (Halfway House, treatment center, detox, extended care, etc.). Other helpful resources to consider:

- local library
- local hospital intake line for psychiatric services
- local mental health center that takes intake phone calls
- local twelve step office

72| Alcohol Rehab Centers

While some recovery-seekers who attend programs also abuse other substances, they consider their primary addiction or drug of choice to be alcohol. Most alcohol rehab programs also offer educational classes and Alcoholics Anonymous meetings. For more information about well-established alcohol rehab programs around the country go to the website for Sober Recovery.

73| Drug Rehab Centers

Drug rehabilitation programs can vary in treatment focus and/or specialty areas. Most drug rehab centers have staff who are trained in substance addiction as a whole, including Certified Alcohol Drug Counselors, doctors, psychiatrists, social workers, case managers, nurses and/or psychologists. These centers focus on a team approach to treatment and often include additional family services. It is not unusual for assessments, individual, group and even couples and family therapy to be offered. Some more expensive facilities may even offer services such as yoga, meditation and nutritional programs. These amenities, while of course nice, are absolutely not essential to the rehabilitation process.

74| California Drug Rehab

California is well-known as a mecca for drug and alcohol treatment facilities. One often hears fetching stories of the "luxuries" of recovering like the stars. While California drug rehab programs may offer top-notch amenities and services, it must be noted that there are plenty of high-quality rehab programs all over the world that do not require one to take out a second mortgage on his/her home. It is not uncommon for recovering addicts to spend thousands upon thousands of dollars for the "best" treatment, and find themselves in a much cheaper and equally useful setting finally getting clean. Much of this has very little to do with the facility and very much to do with the potential recovering person's frame of mind. In fact, for those in rehabilitation who are looking for some sort of rewarding vacation for their addictive patterns, romanticizing this life/death illness may actually prove detrimental to the recovery process.

75| Exclusive Drug Rehabilitation Programs

In a 2004 article, *Forbes Magazine* offered a comprehensive guide to the top luxury rehabilitation programs. These luxury facilities offer high-end spa services, food services and other exclusive amenities that only the wealthiest of recovering addicts can afford. Two of the most expensive and most luxurious of these facilities are Passages in Malibu and Sanctuary in Australia. These treatment facilities can cost upwards of $40,000 per month, and, again, while they may be pleasant, they don't guarantee sobriety. If a person wants to stop using drugs and/or alcohol and to live a more fulfilling life, he/she can do it on the beaches of Malibu and/or in small town Mississippi. Even if you can afford the star treatment, however, you should really take stock of your willingness to seek help before you spend that much money. Willingness to both admit one has a problem and to follow more experienced persons suggestions are by far more important factors to recovery than the surroundings with which one gets.

76| Dual Diagnosis and Treatment

Very common in substance abuse recovery are those clients who are "dually diagnosed." This term means that the person recovering is struggling with both substance addiction and a co-existing mental health disorder, such as depression or anxiety. It is important that recovering addicts with dual diagnosis seek treatment in a facility that offers well-trained practitioners in this area, as recovery from the addiction alone is not enough to create a satiating or even safe lifestyle for such clients. If you are a recovering person and seeking several treatment options, but still suffer from major depressive symptoms, anxiety and/or other related mental disturbances, it is recommended that you seek attention from a medical professional, particularly a psychiatrist, for further examination. There is no reason that anyone should be taking all the necessary steps toward recovery and still feel bad all of the time. If you are interested in learning more about dual diagnosis, treatment and some common mental disorders that co-exist with addictive disorders, visit the website for Dual Diagnosis and Addiction Treatment for further information.

77| Hazelden Rehabilitation Center and Publishing

Those early in recovery may be confused by terms like "conference approved literature" and Hazelden Press. Hazelden is a very expensive and world-renowned drug and alcohol treatment facility located in Minnesota. This organization also has a smaller residential facility in Chicago and owns the premier press company for the manufacture and distribution of recovery literature for sober addicts and professionals. The term "conference approved" means that the literature has been approved for use in twelve-step meetings by the World Service Office of AA. For further information about Hazelden Rehab Center and Publishing, or to purchase more reading and/or educational materials, visit the company's comprehensive website.

78| Residential Living and Recovery

Residential living is sometimes recommended as part of the drug rehabilitation process. Such a decision-making conversation would occur between the inpatient client and his/her treatment team members. Such facilities, like Hazelden in Chicago, while often beneficial, can cost exorbitant amounts of money and are not always an option to people who are just getting sober (in fact, they are most often not an option). While such programs for those in early recovery can prove very helpful in offering a safe haven for living, they are not the only options. Any person who desires sobriety has the option to get sober by attending free Alcoholics Anonymous meetings and/or Narcotics Anonymous meetings and spending most of his/her time with those recovering men and women who are ready and willing to be of service to new members.

79| Mental Illness and Substance Abuse

There are some existing cases where the substance abuse problem seems to be the less causative difficulty in treatment, and the recovering person's mental illness symptoms, such as hallucinations, paranoia, and/or suicidal or homicidal ideation are prevalent. It is not yet known if in such cases it is the severe disturbances in such person's brain functioning that causes the person to abuse substances, or if the addiction began prior to the mental illness. It is known, however, that both substance abuse and other mental illnesses do have a genetic component and that those struggling with severe and/or chronic mental illness and homelessness are the most common population to struggle with substance abuse issues. There are most likely multiple causative relationships for this reality. If you or a loved one is showing symptoms of both severe mental illness and/or substance abuse, it is highly recommended that you visit the website for the National Association for the Mentally Ill (NAMI) where limitless resources and advocacy/educational materials and programming can be found. Help is available for both those struggling with such severe symptoms and their families.

80| Other Treatment Programs

Both Hazelden in Minnesota and The Betty Ford Center in California are well-respected and prominent treatment centers that, while expensive, do not focus on treatment as a luxury, but rather focus on the very basic tenets of treating the addictive thought and behavioral process. Rules and regulations apply to these centers, no matter how famous and/or wealthy the patients, and the focus is on recovery, not on living in luxury. Money goes toward extremely knowledgeable and highly trained professionals who work with clients to "break down" the addictive thought processes and break through denial so that the addict can in fact live a sober life. There are other treatment programs, such as Lakeshore Hospital in Chicago, that offer highly dedicated and trained doctors and social workers, as well as programming for recovering addicts with dual diagnosis. Programs such as this one are far less expensive than those named above, and, if the recovering person is willing, lead to the same end.

81| Changing Unhealthy Environments as Part of the Process of Substance Abuse Recovery

While it is not recommended that a recovering person dismantle all his/her relationships and isolate from the world, it is recommended that he/she recognizes that these environments and situations did not lend themselves to healthy choices or ultimate happiness in life. Most people in early recovery have, in fact, lost a great deal of material things and, more importantly, all of their self-worth. The important thing to remember is that the people who want you to be healthy and safe are truly looking out for your best interests. If people in your life are opposed to your recovery (and this may include certain members of your family) chances are that they are mired in their own illness and/or not available to contribute to your desire for a better life. Remember, if you are not clean and sober, you will lose all those people/things in the long run anyway. Why not try something different?

82| Alcoholics Anonymous

One of the most successful programs in getting alcoholics/addicts sober, when coupled with appropriate detoxification and other support systems (such as outpatient therapy and medication support when needed) is Alcoholics Anonymous. Alcoholics Anonymous is an organization comprised of non-professionals who are each attending meetings, providing support and engaging in a twelve-step practice to both cease substance abuse and treat the emotional malady and emptiness so evident in addiction. Alcoholics Anonymous is completely free and there are meetings all over the world (including other related programs such as Narcotics Anonymous, Alanon, etc.) through which one can receive support. If you are interested in seeking help, contact the local AA office in your nearest major city. There are sober AA members on-call 24 hours a day to answer your questions and to make you feel less isolated and alone.

83| Common Misconceptions About Alcoholics Anonymous

Below are some of the common misconceptions about Alcoholics Anonymous (and related programs) and the correction of these myths.

1. **Alcoholics Anonymous is a religious cult.** While there is a spiritual component to AA (not a religious one), there is no requirement for membership in the fellowship other than a desire to stop drinking. There is no requirement that one believe in anything other than his/her desire to seek help.

2. **If I join AA I will never have a life again.** AA is a program designed to offer a better way of living to those people who have tried their own designs for getting sober and have repeatedly failed at doing so. It is a place where one can meet people with similar experiences, feel understood, and improve his/her quality of life. The purpose is to enhance one's overall life experience-which includes life outside of AA.

3. **AA is anti-medication for members with mental illness** The World Service Office of Alcoholics Anonymous (which is the governing body of rules and regulations for the program) does not indicate anywhere that there is any policy against taking psychotropic medications for mental illness. While there are some members of AA who adhere to this practice, they are not appropriately practicing the tenets of the program outlined by the WSO. AA does not claim to be a group of medical professionals and wholly supports members seeking outside treatment in order to meet their individual needs.

If you have any other questions or concerns about AA and potential aspects that you may feel conflicted about, it is recommended that you directly contact the World Service Office and seek further information.

84| Drug Rehab: The Financial Concern

The kind of drug rehab facilities that are advertised in magazines and on television can be both romanticized and daunting to addicts in early recovery. While these very expensive facilities do have good resources, there are many less expensive facilities that offer strong treatment teams and high-quality care. Additionally, many of the less expensive facilities will also take various insurance plans, including Medicare/Medicaid. The bottom line about drug rehab is that an addict who wants to recover will recover. A person can go to the most prestigious and expensive facility in the world and continue to relapse. Once a person makes up his/her mind that he/she wants help, the options are endless and readily available. Call the nearest major hospital or 12-step office and ask for further information. You can also call the nearest mental health center and ask for intake. Trained case managers should be able to answer your questions.

85| Drug Treatment Centers/Substance Abuse Clinics

"Drug treatment centers" and "substance abuse clinics" are broad terms that can imply several different settings and experiences. Another term one might hear is "substance abuse center." Any similar term is simply a variation on a variety of potential treatment experiences for addicts in early recovery. One of the essential problems with addicts early in recovery is a sense of inflated ego that must be deflated if any help is to be sought, as well as a chemical dependency for which it is essential to receive safe and responsible detox. Drug treatment centers/substance abuse clinics as a whole tend to focus on these two major components in early recovery.

- Inpatient Facility- These centers can be part of a medical facility, a free standing psychiatric facility or exist independently as a place for drug treatment only.
- Halfway Houses- Many addicts enter treatment having lost everything or thinking that they are better than others who are seeking recovery. It is recommended that a newly sober addict, when able, move into such a facility that focuses on sobriety and following rules of society.
- IOP treatment (Inpatient/Outpatient)- This is usually a part of recovery that transpires after the initial inpatient treatment, but this can vary as well. An IOP means that the recovering person is attending daily rigorous educational and treatment-based programming that will help him/her transition from the treatment program to the real world again.

86| Family Support and Addiction Recovery

Many people in early recovery from alcohol and drug abuse have marked family difficulties. This reality exists for a variety of reasons. Alcoholism is a familial disease and one that adversely affects everyone in the person's life. Those around the alcoholic/addict can become unreasonably controlling, angry, nagging and, literally obsessed with the whereabouts and behaviors of the addict. This type of behavior is simply addiction in another form. Obsession with the alcoholic/addict allows those people to escape themselves the same way that the alcoholic/addict is escaping him/herself with substances. For these reasons, it is highly recommended that everyone in the family seek help. Don't be upset, however, if your family members or close friends do not want to seek help along with you. While it is very helpful to a recovering addict if his/her family seeks help, it is certainly not a requirement. Any member of the family can change, providing that he/she is willing to do the necessary work and behave differently. This includes the family members who want help even though the alcoholic doesn't and the alcoholic/addict who desires to stay sober even though the family members want to stay the same.

87| Group Therapy as a Part of Substance Abuse Recovery

Group therapy is becoming more and more popular in the clinical world and there is good reason for this expansion. Group therapy, which is not to be confused with Alcoholics Anonymous, is a group that is comprised of peers who intend to work on relational issues. Sometimes groups include members all struggling with a similar problem, but the more traditional and/or psychodynamic groups involve the formation of relationships within the group context, the reenactment of often self-defeating behavioral patterns, and the resolution of these behaviors/thought processes in a safe, cohesive environment. There is always a clinically trained facilitator in this process. Group therapy can be particularly well-suited for recovering addicts, especially when working with a clinician who understands the underlying workings of the addictive disease, as one of the major difficulties for addicts is the development and maintenance of healthy, supportive and mutual relationships. Group therapy can be a very helpful way to learn about oneself and to also increase the recovering addict's awareness of and relationship with self (the lack of which is the underlying emotional cause of addiction).

88| Individual Therapy as Part of Substance Abuse Recovery

It is often recommended as part of the recovery process that one receive(s) individual therapy to enhance his/her awareness and relational skills. While this can be very helpful, it is important for both incoming addicts and mental health practitioners to know that it is not in the best interest of either the clinician or the client to treat someone who simply refuses to seek additional help for his/her addiction. In fact, treatment under these circumstances may simply enable the user to get worse. That being said, such big decisions must ultimately be left to the discretion of the professional in that therapeutic relationship. Individual therapy is one component of the treatment process that can be very rewarding and useful to those in recovery. If already working with a therapist that you trust, it could certainly be helpful to continue working with him/her as long as you are willing to be open and honest about your addiction treatment and the role that it plays in your life. It is also recommended to consider working with a therapist who has expertise in the field so that you are able to receive the maximum benefits from the energy and time that you invest.

89| Self-Treatment and Addiction Recovery: Why It Doesn't Work

Addiction is a disease of the mind. It is a disease that lies to the addict and convinces him/her, "it is me against the world," and that only the addict has everything under control. Additionally, it is a disease that will actually think two, three or even 20 times about quitting, even after loss and brushes with death have ensued. It is absolutely essential that the person who wants to get sober does not try to do so on his/her own. Staying in the addict brain alone is like trying to be a professional swimmer without arms and legs. It simply cannot work. With additional resources and support, however, both parties can find success.

90| Substance Abuse Education

One of the important factors that many people - both in the field of therapy and in early recovery - neglect is an understanding of the medical and psychological components of the disease of addiction. People often get mired into the logistical, and, of course, essential aspects of treatment but the education regarding how and why a person becomes addicted to drugs is often lost. One major distinction -and mistake- in the treatment of addiction as opposed to other diseases, such as diabetes, is that healthcare practitioners tend to skip the educational component of the treatment. In order to fully respect and understand both the severity of the disease of addiction, as well as the most successful methods of treatment, a person in early recovery, and their families and their current healthcare practitioners who are new to the disease should seek educational opportunities to understand the exact processes that are taking place in the addict's body and mind. The American Council on Drug Addiction website is a good starting place for gathering both information and additional resources. The more timely the research the better, as science is always evolving and new information is always emerging.

91| Finding a Support Network

The number one most recommended network of support for men and women who want to recover from addiction is Alcoholics Anonymous (and related programs, such as Narcotics Anonymous or Cocaine Anonymous). This does not mean that the only place in which a recovering person can seek support is through AA, however. It is recommended that in addition to an active membership in AA, that one also look to the following outlets for support:

- Supportive family members and friends who are either sober or not struggling with any active addiction.
- When possible, some form of individual and/or group therapy can be helpful to both the recovering person and his/her family members.
- Some people have lost their jobs as a result of their addictions. If this is the case, it is recommended that one get in touch with job placement organizations such as Jewish Vocational Services that can help rebuild both one's resume and one's confidence.
- Educational programming/classes on the disease or related difficulties can also be a place to learn and to make connections

92| Coping with Cravings

Cravings for one's drug of choice are an inevitable part of the recovery process. Some people experience cravings only as an early part of the process, and others will have intermittent cravings for the rest of their lives. The difference between a craving, however, and indulging in one's drug of choice, is that the craving can be used as a warning sign that you need to stop and do something to protect yourself against the disease of addiction. Cravings do not generally last more than a minute or two, unless, that is, you allow your mind to indulge in the thought and to become obsessed with the idea of drinking/drugging. Here are some suggestions that can help you, literally, "move your head" to another place BEFORE you take a drink:

- Immediately call sober supports until you reach a person who is available to talk you back to reality.
- Think about all of the rewards you have already gotten in recovery and the fact that you do not wish to lose them for the sake of a drink/drug.
- Start running down the street and release the energy that is consuming your brain. You can also do jumping jacks or run up and down a flight of stairs.
- Clean your car, your office, your apartment. Don't stop until the craving goes away.
- Call someone who may need help, like a sick friend or a lonely neighbor.

Change your environment for the time being-if you are in your apartment, go for a walk. If you are in your office go to the bathroom. The simple act of changing can help shift the mind. It is also suggested that you stay away from "triggers" for use. Triggers can vary with each addict, but can include people, places and even objects, smells or songs.

93| Downsizing in Early Recovery

It is the tendency of many people in early recovery to have the attitude that since they are feeling better, they should add numerous things into their life before being ready. Some of these things can be a new job, a primary romantic relationship, a major move to a far away land, or starting a family. While sometimes such changes are unavoidable, it is strongly recommended that an addict in early recovery spend most of his/her time focusing on getting better. The tendency to "add" comes from the feeling of emptiness that contributed to the addiction in the first place and will most likely lead to increased discontent and may even lead to relapse. It is suggested, although it will feel boring to the recovering addict at first, to keep life as simple and uncomplicated as possible. Recovering from substance abuse is most likely the most difficult thing a person will do in his/her life. No reason to make it more so.

94| Finding Replacement Activities

Finding replacement behaviors for the time the addict spent drinking/drugging may seem like a simple solution, but it can prove to be a very difficult change in which to engage. The addict mind finds normalcy very boring. He/she has most likely lost interest in the simple pleasures of life, such as planting a garden or enjoying a home-cooked meal. Additionally, and often more saddening, is the fact that the person in early recovery has also lost any sense of identity. So what used to be a person that loved to paint or run or go to the theater, has become someone who is miserable any time he/she does not have a drink/drug in hand. These feelings and experiences are both normal and to be expected in early recovery. It is suggested that those in this process be gentle with themselves and stay close to people with more recovery that will instill hope within them again. Additionally, it is highly recommended that no matter how scary or uncomfortable it is, addicts in early recovery find one or two creative/enjoyable outlets to "practice" again. And while, at first, it will feel like you are an actor living another person's life, if you try such simple solutions, there will come a time when your life will feel abundant again.

95| Patience and Recovery

Once a person decides that he/she is ready to get sober it is common to feel a sense of relief, enthusiasm and desire to go back to relationships and situations as though nothing ever happened. Unfortunately, the people who have been subjected to the addict's behavioral storms over and over again are most likely not so ready to be available. Many people will have been so disheartened by repeated, failed promises to change hurtful or even violent behavior from the past, that the recovering addict can be met with less support than he/she might hope. This can be very painful and confusing to an addict in early recovery, but it is also understandable on the other side. In order to deal with such situations, it is suggested that addicts in early recovery not only remain very close to men and women who understand their actual desire to change, but also that they remain patient. As people observe you changing, they will, slowly, learn to trust you again.

96| How to Deal With Others in Recovery

The most difficult thing for recovering addicts to deal with is often relationships with other people. One common mistake people make in early recovery is to assume that everyone in one's recovery program is perfect. The flip side of that is for the addict to think that he/she is better than everyone in their recovery program. These thought processes are common manifestations of the insecurity component of addiction, and neither one is helpful to the recovery process. While it is very helpful to form new relationships with other recovering men and women, it is also important to remember that not only are these simply other human men and women, but they are also other people who are struggling with a severe disease of the mind and body. It can be very scary to be in a group of recovering people who are irritable and moody. The flip side of accepting such behaviors, however, is that people then get to accept you when you are not feeling your best. Additionally, it is suggested that recovering addicts find multiple support systems and friends in the recovery program. While a sponsor in AA is important, one should not become so dependent on him/her (or a handful of people) that he/she feels devastated when they are not readily available. Remember, the addict mind assumes that everyone in the world exists solely for him/her and that anything less than instant gratification is sub-par. With that kind of intense need for attention (which does dissipate over time), it is important that one have numerous people upon whom he/she can rely. And also that if he/she wants others to be patient with him/her, that the same thing should be required in the other direction.

97| Staging an Intervention

The term "interventions" has become a household name in recent years, especially with the emerging popularity of the so-named television show. When important clinical terms get released to the media, however, there is always the potential for misinformation and misinterpretation. The most important thing to remember about interventions for alcohol/drug-related illnesses is that they are intended to impart to the addict, in a loving, non-threatening way the adverse affects that the substance abuse has had on the feelings and lives of friends and family members. Several outcomes are possible during an intervention. First, the addict is very likely to refuse help, feel rage at the family and friends who are challenging his/her escape mechanism, and continue with his/her addiction. Another possible outcome is that the addict will accept treatment as a manipulative way to get out of the intervention and have no intention to follow-through with post-treatment recovery. However, the addict may really respond to loved ones' pleas and feel remorse enough in the moment to accept help.

It is because of this possibility for numerous outcomes that the family and friends who are staging the intervention MUST be prepared to deal with any consequences of this action and willing/ready to follow-through on their words. If not, the intervention will indicate that all members of the addiction system are unwilling to change and, thus, invested in keeping the addict in his/her disease.

If you are interested in staging an intervention or learning more about the process, call Hazelden at 1-800-257-7810 for further information and local contacts.

98| Physical Activity and Recovery

It is likely that when you first get sober that you will find yourself with unimaginable amounts of frenetic energy. It is not uncommon for people in early recovery (even several years in) to have a difficult time sitting for any significant amount of time, remaining attentive for long television programs or conversations, or even sleeping very well. While if these symptoms are out of hand, you should seek medical attention, but understand that this is a normal and expected part of the recovery process. Dr. Diane White of Chicago's Soma Medical Clinic recommends that to obtain and maintain a healthy physical lifestyle, one should engage in the activities he/she enjoyed as a child; such as playing active games or running around the park with a ball. Not only will this help addicts in early recovery feel healthier and more alive, it will help increase a sense of playfulness that has been lost in the abyss of addiction.

99| Positive Thought and Recovery

One of the most highly regarded ways to find peace of mind and contentedness in life is to focus on that which is good. It is common for all people to focus on what they don't have instead of all of the things that they do. This malady is particularly intensified in the alcoholic mind. The focus is generally on deprivation and the fear that there will never be enough alcohol, drugs or (fill in the blank) to go around. It has been seen time and time again that those people who focus on positive thoughts and who even invite the option to think positively about that which makes them uncomfortable will develop a more positive attitude and enjoy a far more fulfilling life experience. Additionally, if a person is focusing on life's abundances, he/she has far less time to think about drinking/drugging.

100| Spirituality and Recovery

One of the major problems with men and women who suffer from addiction is an overwhelming sense of emptiness. There is often a sense that one doesn't belong, has never belonged and that outside forces are essential in order to find any lasting happiness. Unfortunately, such a mindset inevitably leads to either literal or emotional relapse and a sense of loneliness that can pervade addicts long after they stop drinking. In order to find any sense of fulfillment, persons in recovery are asked to identify some sense of spirituality. Spirituality does not mean religion, but, rather, a sense of purpose or connectedness to something other than one's self. Spirituality can include any sense of "otherness" or connectedness through which one finds meaning in life. It can be found through a support system, a connection to nature, a humanistic perspective of the world, through a religion, or even through something like meditation/yoga. The outlet doesn't matter so much as the focus on finding meaning/purpose and a diminishing sense of self-importance. Without this aspect of recovery, most addicts have a very, very difficult time obtaining any long lasting sobriety.

101| The Importance of a Support Network in Recovery

Many people in early recovery wrongfully assume that they will be able to recover alone, without a drug rehab program or support network. By the time a person is ready to seek help for substance addiction, he/she has most likely tried every way imaginable to do so independently of others. These attempts have failed over and over again. The addict mind will lie to its inhabitant over and over and over again until that person either loses every reason to live and/or dies as a result. Some common self-destructive thought processes to watch out for:

- I am so smart that I can intellectualize my way out of the addiction.
- If I read enough self-help literature, I will be able to understand the cause of my addiction and, thus, treat myself.
- Everyone else is wrong and I am right. I can handle this alone.
- If recovery worked, I would already have everything in life I ever wanted. I shouldn't have to work to feel better.
- Why me? Why can't I just drink like everyone else?

It is absolutely recommended that if a person wants to live not only a "dry" life, but a "sober" one, that includes laughter and peace of mind, as well as emotional, relational and financial benefits, that he/she finds a support network right away.

More Titles in the LifeTips Book Series

101 Autism Tips
by Tammi Reynolds

101 Health Insurance Tips
by Michelle Katz

101 Student Loan Tips
by Jennifer Mathes

101 Sports Apparel Tips
by Heidi Splete

Breinigsville, PA USA
09 November 2010
249061BV00004B/2/A

9 781602 750296